Tinsel Talk

Fakery or Pleasantry?

Ronda Chervin, Ph.D.

En Route Books and Media, LLC
Saint Louis, MO

ENROUTE
Make the time

En Route Books and Media, LLC
5705 Rhodes Avenue
St. Louis, MO 63109

Contact us at
contactus@enroutebooksandmedia.com

Cover Credit: Sebastian Mahfood using DALL-E

ISBN-13: 979-8-88870-549-0
Library of Congress Control Number:
Available online at https://catalog.loc.gov

“It is the wisdom of this world to conceal one’s feelings behind pretense and veil one’s meaning with words, to show things that are false to be true and to show what is true to be fallacious.

It is the wisdom of the righteous, on the other hand, to have no pretense, to use words to mean and not to hide meaning, to love the truth as it is and to avoid falsehood.”

(The Moral Reflections on Job
by Pope St Gregory the Great)

"It is the wisdom of this world to conceal one's feelings behind pretense and veil one's meaning with words, to show things that are false to be true and to show what is true to be fallacious.

It is the wisdom of the righteous, on the other hand, to have no pretense, to use words to mean and not to hide meaning, to love the truth as it is and to avoid falsehood."

(The Moral Reflections on Job
by Pope St Gregory the Great)

What's Inside?

Why I Wrote *Tinsel Talk*

Perpetual annoyance!

Tinsel is a decorative sparkling piece of cloth. By 'tinsel' used in this little book, I am referring to the secondary meaning of tinsel: something superficially attractive or glamorous but of little real worth, or fake.

Examples will explain. In ordinary language, of everyday conversational, lingo, I hear one word or phrase after another that seems to me to be fake.

"Ladies and Gentlemen" on the doors of public toilets – the word Lady and the word Gentlemen originally referred to those of the noble classes in Europe. So how many who walk through those doors are of the noble classes?

"Have a great day!" Great used to refer to something over and above good, some stupendous reality or happening such as a great ocean or a great performance of a singer. Now it seems to mean more that someone hopes I will have a day free from any frustrations!

"Hello, sweetie pie," addressed, even by me, to a pet who enters the room. In what way is a cat or a dog a pie or sweet?

The form of "tinsel talk" that is most frequent is what is called euphemism. This is defined by the Oxford Language Dictionary as:

> "A mild or indirect word or expression substituted for one considered to be too harsh or blunt when referring to something unpleasant or embarrassing."

As an example, that dictionary provides this one: "instead of describing firing many employees as 'cutting the staff' it is called 'downsizing.'"

Now, you might say, what's wrong with such a euphemism?

I would say that downsizing makes it sound as if there are no innocent victims of the decision of the managers of the company. The older expression, cutting the staff, clearly implies a definite hurtful choice.

With each of the examples I will bring forward in *Tinsel Talk*, I will run the words through this format:

- The words
- Why they seem fake
- How using them may be out of a desire to make life seem more pleasant than it is
- The way the particular words may have evolved over decades or even centuries
- Reasons why to use that word(s) or not to.

You may be thinking why in the world would Ronda Chervin think it is important to even try to figure this all out. Some sort of 'demon' of criticalness or even churlishness?

I have asked myself that question often. Here is the reason I think writing about *Tinsel Talk: Fakery or Pleasantry* is, after all, worth a try:

Love of truth! When we use tinsel talk thoughtlessly all through the day, we begin to need to use additional words to get at truth.

Example: If wishing someone a great day, only means one free of frustration, then to talk about true greatness, we have to put in something like:

"This is REALLY great."

Or to commend someone for being truly sweet we would have to explain:

"I call you sweetie pie in fondness, but you REALLY are sweet."

Another reason for exploring tinsel talk, I think, is that some people, usually unconsciously, become so fed up with such fake phrases that they go overboard with nasty words. I know many people who use these words sometimes more than 10 times a day:

Sh*t
f*ck
*ss-h*le!

Of course, there are other reasons for using vulgar words, such as being kind of addicted to anger, expressed in this way.

Consider, in the 1970's some Catholic spiritual guides told us that it would be good for us if we changed our language:

Instead of saying "I'm angry, I hate you," say "What you just said made me feel uncomfortable."

Now, that seemed very good to me, except that using the pleasanter word uncomfortable didn't express the anger.

But, with regard to vulgarity, the “S-word,” and the “F-word,” when angered, absolutely expresses anger, so the person one is upset with gets it loud and clear.

In any case, this booklet is not a definitive philosophy of language, but more exploratory in the realm of spirituality of daily life.

A co-author of mine into contemporary spirituality suggested that it might be form of “mindfulness.” Mindfulness means maintaining a moment-by-moment awareness of our thoughts, feelings, bodily sensations, and surrounding environment.

As I set forth, here is my prayer:

> Jesus, the Word, who proclaimed that “the truth will set you free,” help us in each moment to use words in a way that is not fakely pleasant or rude, but in a loving way.

Mentally Unbalanced vs. Crazy

Here are excerpts from the Oxford dictionary set of definitions:

1. mentally deranged, especially manifested in a wild or aggressive way. "Stella went crazy and assaulted a visitor."

   Similar: mad, insane, out of one's mind, lunatic, mad as a hatter, nutty, cuckoo, loony…
   Opposite: Sane

2. extremely enthusiastic.
   "I'm crazy about Cindy.

   Similar: passionate, fanatical, excited, wild
   Opposite: apathetic, indifferent

So, in the case of the first meaning of crazy, why does using the words mentally unbalanced seem fake? Especially in the use of the word crazy to describe someone potentially violently insane, mentally unbalanced surely doesn't convey the same idea.

But, for sure, the words 'mentally unbalanced' are more pleasant.

Why, then, has this euphemism become more and more popular?

It seems the word crazy has become associated with those so insane that they must be locked up in asylums.

I am thinking that psychiatrists working in such institutions used many different words for specific states of insanity, such as schizophrenic, paranoid, bi-polar. So crazy would be too broad a word for them to use.

How then are we to speak of people in the work-place, in our places of worship, or even more, in our own homes, who were unbalanced in some ways but not crazy in the sense of insane?

In those cases, isn't it more charitable, loving, to refer to some such person not as crazy but as mentally unbalanced?

Come to think of it, in the past the distinction was made between psychotic and neurotic with neurotic being milder. More like what we now call mentally unbalanced?

Here is why I think it is better not to use the word "crazy." I have a dear friend who has been mentally ill all her life, exacerbated by sexual abuse of several brothers when she was a child.

For short times, she has been put into an institution, but mostly she lives a fairly normal life with the help of a psychiatrist, medicines, support groups, and priest-mentors.

Whenever I happened to use the word crazy about anyone, it would cause her deep pain. Finally, she told me how she associated the word with being bullied at school.

Would I do her the favor of not using the word crazy casually?

How about eccentric? Is that a softer word for crazy? Not exactly. Eccentric is defined as: unconventional, slightly strange.

For example, a person might choose for fun to wear shoes that don't match – a sneaker and a dress shoe.

Underlying the whole question of fakery vs. pleasantry with regard to the word crazy, I think that those who have severe mental problems can feel ostracized, shamed, despised and inferior.

Anything we can do in the way of milder labelling to help such people, clearly will not be no fakery but a form of love.

My prayer:

> Dear Creator God, we do not know why you permit that some humans are more sane or balanced than others. We thank you for whatever is sane and balanced in a good way in ourselves and those in our families. About anything "crazy," as described in the past, or mentally unbalanced in ourselves or in others, we beg you to send healing graces. May we or they feel that love in the language we use.

How are you? And Have a Great Day!

You are probably so familiar with these forms of greeting and goodbye that it would be hard to imagine that anyone hated to hear them.

Why?

I like to say that if everyone you asked told you how they *really* were when you asked, "How are you?" you could never do anything else with your day but listen to their tales of woe!

So how fake is the question "How are you?"

And, as I mentioned in the introduction, "Have a great day!" is fake because "great" is such an ambiguous word. We don't really mean that most of the people we meet can have a great day in the sense of stupendous or amazingly full of achievement!

On the other hand, listen to my opposite experience with "How are you?" I had suggested to students in my course on Philosophy of Love, that they try being more sincere by not asking "How are you?" when they had no interest in hearing a real answer.

However, after a few days we went back to "How are you?"

Why?

Because we had to realize that whereas "How are you?" is often fake, not saying anything to an acquaintance or friend seems positively unfriendly – unpleasant!

"Have a *great* day!" seems to have replaced "Have a *nice* day!" Maybe this is because whereas the word 'nice' used to be a pleasant word, gradually, from over-use perhaps, it became the opposite of terrific. Telling someone that her dress looked 'nice' became a way of politely telling them you thought that dress was ugly!

So, what is the alternative here between fakery and pleasantry? Here is what seems to me to be loving instead:

I say, "God bless you," instead of "How are you?" And if I really want to know how the person is, I make sure to stand still and wait for a real answer.

Instead of "Have a great day!" I like to say, "God bless your day."

Dear God of love, thank you for all those we love and even those acquaintances whose presence, even in passing, is welcome. Holy Spirit, inspire each of us in our own way to find ways of greeting that are not conventional mutterings, but real expressions of love.

Diminutives or Catastrophic Lingo

Diminutives and Catastrophics are opposite forms of "tinsel talk" as in calling a 60 year old daughter "my little chickidee" and a King in a deck of cards "hubby!"

Diminutives are words which convey the smallness of an object, but also a sense of intimacy and endearment, says Wikipedia.

Catastrophic: Exaggerated descriptions of objects, events, feelings such as:

> "I am dying of the heat" (at 75 degrees), or
> "It's the end of the world!" Because the political party one hates just won the election.

Both diminutives and catastrophic language aren't literally true. In that sense their use is fakery.

Are they pleasant?

Clearly yes, in the case of diminutives. An old mother gets joy out of remembering when she called her now old daughter a "little chickadee."

I ask myself, why I think such charming lingo is fatuous (a fancy word for silly and sentimental).

Is my critical spirit a way of coming against my tears because, as an old woman now, I suffer from the loss of a young son and a middle-aged daughter of mine?

Probably so. At the same time diminutives could also be a way of dealing with the fear that those now old children will one day take over and boss the old mother around in role reversal!

In the case of catastrophic lingo, the pleasure is more subtle. We can't control the weather, but saying we are dying of the heat or the cold, conveys the illusion that we can blame the weather for our discomfort. Blaming is an active response, pleasanter than just sweating it out!

Saying that it is the end of the world because that party won, conveys the illusion that they will not enjoy their victory, since the end of the world will take place first!

On the other hand, would it really be better if the mother addressed her 60-year-old son with the words:

> "Greetings my old son – soon to become as decrepit as I am."

> Or, is it better to assassinate the elected officials from the party we voted against?

I am exaggerating.

What, then, is the loving way with respect to diminutives and catastrophic expressions?

Here are some possibilities:

> "God bless you, my dear son. I have loved you since your childhood. Recall, I used to describe you as "my little duckie." Now you are a strong older man whom I trust to lean on in my elderly years."

(In conversation with political allies) "How sad it is that we lost and they won. What can we learn from this for our work in the next election? How can get more of our people into the Senate and the House in the mid-term elections?"

What are loving ways you can think of in the areas of diminutives or catastrophic lingo?

My prayer:

God, our Father, you created us with the gift of speech. You want us to use words in ways that are creative and sometimes funny. If patterns we have fallen into are not as loving as they could be, please help us talk better.

Don't Stick me in a Box!

I am much into personality typologies – Myers-Briggs, the Enneagram, and the 4 Temperaments.

A friend who dislikes these theories accused me of always labelling people. She especially dislikes when I label her as in:

Since you're a sanguine, naturally you always think that things will turn out well, but usually they don't!

Or, since you're a Myers-Briggs "P" (flexible play it by ear) naturally you can't bear to plan ahead, but I need to plan ahead in detail, because I am a "J."

"Don't stick me in a box!" is her response to such labelling as I do kind of automatically. I have been trying to desist from blurting out these theories when talking to her.

Why do I like typologies? These started to become popular among Catholics in the '70's when psychology became more accepted.

What I like best about them is that it helps me accept differences. I have to realize that it is as hard for someone who deals with life's uncertainties by playing it by ear, to keep rigid time schedules, as it is for me, who deals with these uncertainties by obsessive planning for every possibility to let go and see what happens!

However, a relative of mine likes to say, "Ronda, character is not fate." She sees my use of these typologies as a way of excusing myself for all my annoying extreme forms of choice. As in, Ronda, stop nagging me to plan ahead on everything with the excuse that you are a planner-type.

In the meantime, I have been thinking about the other woman's admonition: "Don't stick me in a box."

Is this image itself of sticking someone into a box by labelling a form of fakery? Surely, I don't literally put anyone into a paper storage box!

It seems to me not so much fakery as using a suggestive metaphor.

Metaphor is defined as: a figure of speech in which a word or phrase is applied to an object or action to which it is not literally applicable.

Now, then, however, is accusing someone of sticking one in a box when the speaker is only trying to describe one's usual patterns of behavior really the most loving response?

As in, could it be kind of prideful to think that "I am such a totally individual person that nothing I do fits under any label"?

On the other hand, could labeling be a form of avoiding the labor of relating to friends and acquaintances as individuals in favor of quickly writing them off as this or that type opposite to one's own?

There might be several reasons others dislike being labelled. But it is surely more charitable for me not to label anyone in his/her own hearing if they will feel stuck in a box!

My prayer:

Dear Creator God, You have made us unique persons but also with lots of common traits. Help us to evaluate each encounter with others to see what is most loving. Sometimes to analyze types, but other times to go with the flow out of love!

Hyperbole

Hyperbole is defined as exaggerated_statements or claims not meant to be taken literally.

Examples?

"You're my best friend," told to 5 different people!

"Be there in a jiffy," really in a half hour.

"God damn you!" meaning only "Shut up, don't bother me!"

It would seem that one would get used to the lingo of those who use hyperbole. Why get upset?

If we are used to taking people at their word, then we could often be disappointed, or upset unnecessarily.

To me, the words "best friend" mean someone I could talk to every day by phone or text or e-mail. But someone with 5 best friends might only mean that I could have access to her/him once a week max!

To me, a jiffy means 5 minutes. So, waiting impatiently outside the house for 30 minutes for a ride from someone can be frustrating. It feels as if "*Your* time counts and you were doing whatever came up before driving to my house and you don't care about *my* wasted time!"

"God damn you," when more people were strong Christians or Catholics actually meant that you wanted someone to go to hell! But if you use that expression simply as a cultural little negative, I shouldn't be upset over nothing.

Even more important is the use of hyperbole in Scripture. Some scholars think that hyperbole was common in those times.

Examples:

> Some scholars think that Christ was using hyperbole just when He spoke of a plank being in one's eye while attempting to remove the splinter in a brother's eye. (Matthew 7:3-5)
>
> Or, when Jesus tells us that "If your right eye causes you to stumble, pluck it out and cast it from you." (Matt. 5 :29),
>
> There is a story by Flannery O'Connor where one of the characters pricks out an eye based on taking Scripture literally. She uses this far-out tale to illustrate why some Protestant Christians are wrong to insist on Sola Scriptura.

Such examples make me think that I needn't consider hyperbole, in itself, to be a form of fakery.

On the other hand, some Catholics seem to think that they can dismiss mentions of hell by Jesus as just hyperbole! They believe that most people go right to heaven because hell is just a threat to get us to obey the Lord!

It says in the New Testament that all those who were ill who came to see Jesus were healed. Does "all" mean literally every single one – even those with colds or toothaches???

This matter is important because some lose their faith in God when they pray for healing and they are not healed. If Jesus told us that all our prayers would be answered, why not that prayer?

I am not a Scripture scholar. My view about this is that answered prayers don't mean in the way we wish, but in an ultimate sense – if we follow Jesus there will be no illness or pain in heaven. We need to have faith that Jesus *could* heal us right now, just as he did when He lived on earth. But we don't need to doubt that Jesus is real because His answer is sometimes "wait."

I remind myself that Scripture is not philosophy. One can prove in philosophy that literally omnipotence = *all* powerfulness…or that *all* killing of the innocent is murder.

But in the language of the Bible many terms are general rather than literal – we don't have planks of wood in our eyes when we judge splinters in the eyes of others!

My prayer:

> Holy Spirit, sometimes it all seems too complex for me. I want to just have blind faith and give up analyzing things. However, we have been taught that faith needs to seek understanding. Help us not to use hyperbole in deceptive ways, but only in good ways.

Mid-Tinsel Talk-Self-Examination

The more I write, the more I am tempted to think that the whole topic is overly critical and churlish.

Why?

I can't help noticing that some of my family and friends are so much better than I am in other ways than lingo. Is this treatise, then, a way for me to 'say' to them, even if they never read it, my talk is better than yours? To try to "take the splinter" out of their eyes when there is a "plank" in my eye?

However, the Holy Spirit might be telling me that the answer is to write the rest of the booklet more in the form of self-examination????

I will keep going and see how it feels.

Unattractive vs. Ugly

One of the ugliest words in the English language is probably ugly! Onomatopoeic is a term for words that sound like what they mean – examples are sizzle or ding-dong! So, ugly sounds ugly.

Casually used to describe a pile or dirt or a bruise, it becomes insulting when describing the way a person looks or acts.

How wounding it is to a child to be considered ugly by family members or classmates! There is nothing one can do about being the shortest of 3 boys or having a longer than usual nose, short of an expensive face-lift.

Isn't it more pleasant and, really, more loving to describe something as unattractive or less attractive or not so attractive rather than ugly?

Or, if someone asks you if you like the dress they are wearing to say, "that color is attractive on you," vs. "you really look ugly in that dress!"

Is there a negative to such euphemisms as unattractive for ugly?

The only one I can see is that by now such pleasant words are so common that I hardly trust any compliments.

What about shaming names for the ugliness of being too fat such as fatty or fatso?

When I used to hear someone describe another person as "overweight," I would think: "Why not tell it like it is? He/she is fat!"

But sometimes a euphemism becomes itself a nasty word. A woman I know who is overweight pointed out to me that by now that word is offensive. One has to say something like – it could benefit your health if you lost a few pounds.

But then I wondered if applauding the euphemism as charitable might be a way of avoiding the stress of trying to help people to honestly deal with negatives. When I think of someone as benefiting by losing a few pounds vs. fat, am I shrugging off the possibility that such a one is pretty near to becoming so obese as to be at risk about health issues? And, therefore, perhaps, needs a strong confrontation from me if I truly love him or her?

At the same time negative nicknames can make it seem as if that bodily characteristic was the essence of that individual. Clearly uncharitable.

My prayer:

> Oh, dear Jesus, we hope never to shame and offend others for things they cannot help about themselves. What about unattractive things that are partly our own fault such as being too fat? May we accept shaming names as an incentive to beg for the grace to overcome addictions.

'Just' do this – and Tech

Would you believe that one of the most frequent sins I bring to the Sacrament of Confession is yelling at techies for using the word "just!"

What?

Many in my family are techies. They try to help me solve computer problems that hold up my work. I do okay until a mentor throws in the word "just" as in

"Now, dear Ronda, JUST hit that button on the right."

"Aaaargh," I growl, "I don't see any button!"

"Not on the screen, the one on the slab at the bottom."

"Grrrrrr!" How would I know what you meant. I hate computers. I'm throwing this one into the lake right now."

"Listen, Ronda, if you start yelling at me, I'm not going to help you any more today."

"Okay but just don't say "just" as if it was a simple easy matter.

I like to say that learning tech for 80-year-olds is as hard as it would be for a horseman in 1900 to get into a car without any lessons and drive well!

So, when a techie says to one of us oldies, "just do this or that" does that make the word "just" fake?

From years of resenting the word "just" in tech matters, I realize that it is a more of a generation gap problem.

Why not "just" thank the techie and get on with it?

My prayer:

> Holy Spirit, how grateful I am to You for helping techies to invent, utilize, and teach techniques. I am glad for all the ways I have been able, with their help, to do the work I do for promoting Your kingdom. Help, help, help, me to be more patient with techies and with myself as a slow, slow, learner.

"Losing" Loved ones vs. they Died

Oscar Wilde, the famous 19th century playwright, had an old woman speak this line about another woman twice widowed:

"It's one thing to lose one husband, but surely it is careless to lose two!"

For several decades I have noticed that the use of the word "dead" is taboo. Almost everyone in the US speaks of death of others as "loss."

The positive side is that bereavement ministry is now so often a way to cope with the death of loved ones. When we hear of the death of someone's closest and dearest, we rush to empathize with the grief of loss.

However, I dislike the term "loss" because it sounds like even Christians seem to have insufficient belief and hope of being reunited with the one who died in heaven one day. Catholics believe that unless they were terrible sinners who never repented, they will probably be in Purgatory and then forever, an infinite amount of time, in Heaven. And we hope to be with them "together forever," as I like to say.

But, but, but, someone might reply…the word "dead" sounds so final. "Loss" sounds more as if they could be found again.

These aspects seem to be better combined when we use words such as "passed on," "taken by Jesus," "went home."

I also like to say when I hear of the death of someone' spouse: the degree of grief is the degree of love…those in unhappy marriages don't feel loss, they feel liberated!

Unusual, but real, are instances where a couple was so close that after one has gone home to Jesus the other one experiences his/her spouse vibrantly present in their home. Not "loss" really.

My prayer:

Jesus, we recite in the Creed that we believe in the resurrection of the dead. Help us at the time when a beloved person leaves this earth to pray for their souls to go to You and that we may follow You so closely as to be reunited to them in Your home.

Issues vs. Problems

In the last decade I have noticed, in ordinary conversation, that the word "problem" rarely occurs. Instead, everything difficult is considered an "issue."

Pondering the matter, I thought that in some way issue is a euphemism, a more pleasant word, than problem. Problem is a heavy word. Issue sounds more something with many possible outcomes.

Example:

"I'm have an issue about buying a new car." Hearing this, a friend is likely to reply: "Oh, maybe I can help you."

"I have a problem about buying a new car," sounds more like maybe someone doesn't have enough credit to buy one.

Or

"I have an issue with our evening schedule," sounds as if the spouse could reply, "Not a biggie. Let's look at the way the week usually goes and decide what to change."

"I have a problem with our evening schedule," could call forth an answer from the spouse like,

"Problem, eh? Well, the real problem is that when you started going to a happy hour at the bar for 2 hours before coming home, everything is so delayed that....!"

So, again, is the word "issue" fake for "problem" or simply a more pleasant word?

Fake if the difference implies that big, serious, problems are going to be brushed under the table, but pleasant if it is a way to avoid sinking under seemingly unsolvable problems.

My prayer:

> We wish we had neither problems or issues, but we know that to be Christian is to accept the crosses that we cannot remove. If there are ways to resolve problems/issues that will help us, please, Holy Spirit, help us to find them!

Unconditional Love vs. Prophetic Love

Some Christians were brought up so strictly that they never think of God as Love, only as the Judge. To counteract such fear, it has been common in the last decades for preachers and teachers to assure us of God's unconditional love.

It sounds good. God doesn't hate the sinner and enjoy thinking of plunging him/her into hell one day. He doesn't sit on a throne with a scorecard.

Just the same I don't find the word "unconditional" in Scripture. I find that the love of God for us always includes deep sorrow over our sins and the wish that we would turn to Him for grace to change.

The analogy is often made to good parental love. We do not tell the child, "If you don't do exactly what I say, I will hate you and reject you and throw you out of the house." That would be very conditional love.

However, if the child interprets unconditional love to mean that he/she can do anything no matter how wrong and hurtful without fear of punishment, is that good? It used to be called "spoiling" a child.

I am thinking a term for the right kind of love of an authority, whether God or a parent, for a son/daughter, might be called "prophetic love."

Out of love for us God sent prophets to admonish and warn us. That was not because God hated us.

"Hate the sin, love the sinner," was the great way St. Augustine taught this point.

So unconditional should mean, God loves us always, but never in the sense that God doesn't care how we hurt others and ourselves by our sins and defects.

My prayer:

> Holy Spirit, I wish that all preachers and teachers would make the distinctions in this treatise. May we bask in the forever love of God but always retain the "fear of God" that is awe in His true justice.

Heavy drinker vs. Drunk or Alcoholic

Calling another a "drunk" is certainly shaming. Using a more pleasant label such as "heavy drinker," or "someone with a drinking problem," is surely more loving.

However, the use of the more pleasant word could feed into what is called "denial."

"Don't call me a drunk or an alcoholic even… I am only a heavy drinker."

In Alcoholics Anonymous, members are told to admit that they are alcoholics.

Does that mean other people who know that person should so label them…or isn't it better that others use euphemisms such as "heavy drinker"? More charitable?

A counselor suggested to me that a way of talking that is not shaming but doesn't foster denial could be like this:

"Tell me dear friend, how much do you drink each day and when?"

"Early in the morning?" Is that really good for you?"

Talking about someone as a drunk or an alcoholic to another person falls under detraction, unless there is a pastoral reason?

Huh?

Calumny is telling lies. Detraction is telling the truth but in such a way that another person will think less of the one we are talking about. A pastoral reason would be to warn a teen against hanging out with a group of friends who spend every night at the bar.

Prayer:

> Dear Father God, you created many things to give us pleasure and relaxation. Abuse is when we over-do in such a way that we harm ourselves and possibly others, as in drinking too much when planning to drive. We thank you for all the programs to counter-act addictions of all kinds. We thank you for all those we know well or don't know who have been helped to open to Your grace to be free of addiction.

Other "Tinsel Talk" Expressions

My father put together a treatise on euphemisms. That was way back in the '70's.

I would like to put down here some of his and some I have found, but only in brief, since I am sure that by now you get the concept: Fakery or Pleasantry, sometimes one, sometimes the other, but try to speak with charity.

Ladies and Gentlemen vs. Toilets

I already wrote about this one. I was amazed to discover from watching toddlers that they usually think urine and bowels are fun, cute things! That is why it takes so much effort to toilet train them.

Since we are so accustomed to such euphemisms as bathroom, restroom, Ladies and Gentlemen, it could be unlovingly offensive to insist that other people only use the blunt word "toilet."

By making little jokes about whether my friends are really Ladies or Gentlemen in the sense of noble women and men, I like to get people thinking.

My plan is to use toilet myself often, but not try to persuade others to do so!

"Chill out" vs. "Relax"

Sounds fake to me! Yes, chill out if one means escaping from torrid weather or bodily heat from gymnastics. But, if it only means relax because one is too stressed, why not put it more simply as "relax?" I certainly don't want to "chill out" because I am stressed out from being out in 20 below zero weather!

"Overly-concerned" vs. "Bossy"

If we were all humble we wouldn't mind being bossed around, would we? True as that might be from a Christian point of view, surely being bossy isn't a virtue.

Bossy people love to domineer over others telling them what to do, if possible every minute of the day! We do this in the name of lovingly helping others with their issues, oops, problems. With bossy women this is sometimes called being a "smother-mother" or an "umbrella mother."

Clearly it is more pleasant to tell someone not to be overly concerned than to accuse them of being bossy.

What would be a loving way to deal with bossiness in oneself and others?

Perhaps to approach the bossy person with words such as these:

> "Dear friend or mother or father of grown children, it saddens me that you are so concerned about me, even about trivial daily matters. It comes from love, but it makes me feel as if I was still a little kid with no good judgement of my own. Would you be willing to try not giving me advice unless I ask for it, unless I am doing something really dangerous?"

"Unmotivated" vs. "Lazy"

Sloth is the name of one of the 7 deadly sins that we usually call laziness.

Myself energetic about lots of tasks, I usually look down on what seem laziness in others. However, I have had to admit that more laid-back people are usually happier than workaholics like me!

Besides, I can be lazy about chores which those lazy people apply themselves to better than I do, such as housework.

Here is a humorous example of the loving way a mother chided her messy, slobbish teens:

One day instead of trying to shame them into becoming tidier, she walked into their bedroom and applauded them with these words: "Gee, you keep your ceiling neat!"

I have found thinking of those less energetic as less motivated helps me find ways to challenge them.

Instead of saying, "Gee, Jane, those trash bags are overflowing – soon we will have rats in the kitchen," I might say, "I love the way the kitchen looks when the trash bags have been taken to the dump." Or "It's funny, but I have this love of taking trash out, good exercise, nice looking kitchen. Would you let me have that job?"

Being called "Young Lady" when I am an "Old Woman"

I have written several books about aging in a Christian way. I try to teach readers to come against the idolization of youthfulness. Shouldn't we be happy that we are first Half-way to Eternity, and finally 9 Toes in Eternity?

How fake is it to address a 60-year-old woman as a young lady?

On the other hand, would I like someone to address me as "Hello, old hag?" Actually, the word "hag" is good in its derivation. It was the word used for the old widows who prayed for the martyrs in the Roman arena!

What is the loving alternative to the fake word or the offensive word "old?"

How about telling young people that we enjoy their youthfulness and telling older people that we love to see their wise faces. A young person might tell a grandmother, "I envy you, being closer to eternal life."

"Overly-Talkative" vs. "Blabbermouth"

Since I happen to be a blabbermouth myself, I kind of expect others to upbraid me for this fault. One spiritual director asked me to check out how many times I use the word "I" at the start of my sentences when talking with others!

Once retired from teaching where I had every right to be extremely talkative, I became ashamed of this trait. I wrote a booklet entitled *Talkaholics!* You might want to check it out.

Imagine the battlefield when I talk with friends who are also blabbermouths!

So, sure call me out politely as being overly-talkative, but I don't mind if you say, "Shut up a few minutes, so I can get a word in edgewise."

Lord, have mercy.

Last Loving Thoughts

"Speak the truth with love!" (Ephesians 4:15)

"You're on the ball!" So, is this little treatise on the ball? Is "on the ball" fakery, pleasantry or a suggestive metaphor of loving praise?

www.ingramcontent.com/pod-product-compliance
Lightning Source LLC
La Vergne TN
LVHW040221110826
845146LV00005B/1374